The New Nest

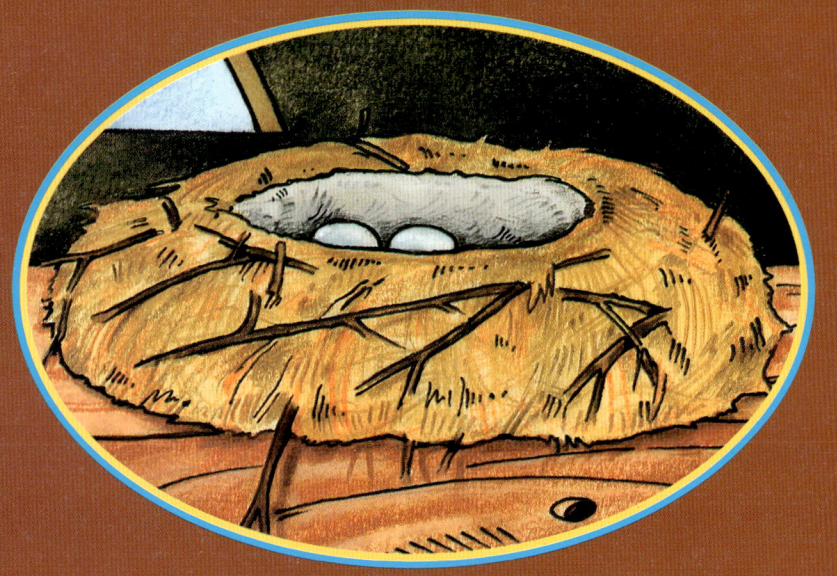

Written by
Sandra Iversen

Illustrated by
Peter Paul Bajer

Mother Bird and Father Bird
went to the field.
Father Bird looked
under some big trees.
He got some twigs.
He took the twigs back to the roof.

Mother Bird looked
under some little trees.
She got some twigs.
She took the twigs back to the roof.

Mother Bird and Father Bird made a nest.

"We need some straw for the nest," said Mother Bird.
"Where will we get some straw?" said Father Bird.

"We need some wool for the nest," said Mother Bird.
"Where will we get some wool?" said Father Bird.

Mother Bird and Father Bird twisted the wool and the straw into the twenty twigs.

"The nest is ready," said Mother Bird. "Now I can lay my eggs!"